As a Man Thinketh

AND

Out From the Heart

AND

Morning and Evening Thoughts

James Allen.

THE BEST OF JAMES ALLEN

INCLUDES

As a Man Thinketh

AND

Out From the Heart

AND

Morning and Evening Thoughts

By

James Allen

Mind is the Master power that moulds and makes,
And Man is Mind, and evermore he takes
The tool of Thought, and, shaping what he wills,
Brings forth a thousand joys, a thousand ills:—
He thinks in secret, and it comes to pass:
Environment is but his looking-glass.

PUBLISHED BY

SEAWOLF
PRESS

THE BEST OF JAMES ALLEN
Copyright ©2019 by SeaWolf Press

EDITION INFORMATION
The text is taken from a 1913 Thomas Crowell edition.

SeaWolf Press
P.O. Box 961
Orinda, CA 94563
Email: support@seawolfpress.com
Web: http://www.SeaWolfPress.com

FOREWORD

THIS little volume (the result of meditation and experience) is not intended as an exhaustive treatise on
the much-written-upon subject of the power of thought.
It is suggestive rather than explanatory, its object being to stimulate men and women to the discovery and
perception of the truth that—

"They themselves are makers of themselves."

by virtue of the thoughts, which they choose and encourage; that mind is the master-weaver, both of the inner
garment of character and the outer garment of circumstance, and that, as they may have hitherto woven in ignorance and pain they may now weave in enlightenment
and happiness.

JAMES ALLEN.

BROAD PARK AVENUE,
ILFRACOMBE,
ENGLAND

CONTENTS

As a Man Thinketh

Out From the Heart

As a Man Thinketh

THOUGHT AND CHARACTER

THE aphorism, "As a man thinketh in his heart so is he," not only embraces the whole of a man's being, but is so comprehensive as to reach out to every condition and circumstance of his life. A man is literally *what he thinks,* his character being the complete sum of all his thoughts.

As the plant springs from, and could not be without, the seed, so every act of a man springs from the hidden seeds of thought, and could not have appeared without them. This applies equally to those acts called "spontaneous" and "unpremeditated" as to those, which are deliberately executed.

Act is the blossom of thought, and joy and suffering are its fruits; thus does a man garner in the sweet and bitter fruitage of his own husbandry.

"Thought in the mind hath made us, What we are
By thought was wrought and built. If a man's mind
Hath evil thoughts, pain comes on him as comes
The wheel the ox behind. . .

 . . If one endure
In purity of thought, joy follows him
As his own shadow—sure."

Man is a growth by law, and not a creation by arti-
fice, and cause and effect is as absolute and undeviating
in the hidden realm of thought as in the world of visible
and material things. A noble and Godlike character is
not a thing of favor or chance, but is the natural result
of continued effort in right thinking, the effect of long-
cherished association with Godlike thoughts. An ignoble
and bestial character, by the same process, is the result
of the continued harbouring of grovelling thoughts.

Man is made or unmade by himself; in the armory
of thought he forges the weapons by which he destroys
himself; he also fashions the tools with which he builds
for himself heavenly mansions of joy and strength
and peace. By the right choice and true application of
thought, man ascends to the Divine Perfection; by the
abuse and wrong application of thought, he descends below the level of the beast. Between these two extremes
are all the grades of character, and man is their maker
and master.

Of all the beautiful truths pertaining to the soul
which have been restored and brought to light in this
age, none is more gladdening or fruitful of divine promise and confidence than this—that man is the master of
thought, the moulder of character, and the maker and
shaper of condition, environment, and destiny.

As a being of Power, Intelligence, and Love, and the
lord of his own thoughts, man holds the key to every
situation, and contains within himself that transforming and regenerative agency by which he may make
himself what he wills.

Man is always the master, even in his weaker and most abandoned state; but in his weakness and degradation he is the foolish master who misgoverns his "household." When he begins to reflect upon his condition, and to search diligently for the Law upon which his being is established, he then becomes the wise master, directing his energies with intelligence, and fashioning his thoughts to fruitful issues. Such is the *conscious* master, and man can only thus become by discovering *within himself* the laws of thought; which discovery is totally a matter of application, self analysis, and experience.

Only by much searching and mining, are gold and diamonds obtained, and man can find every truth connected with his being, if he will dig deep into the mine of his soul; and that he is the maker of his character, the moulder of his life, and the builder of his destiny, he may unerringly prove, if he will watch, control, and alter his thoughts, tracing their effects upon himself, upon others, and upon his life and circumstances, linking cause and effect by patient practice and investigation, and utilizing his every experience, even to the most trivial, everyday occurrence, as a means of obtaining that knowledge of himself which is Understanding, Wisdom, Power. In this direction, as in no other, is the law absolute that "He that seeketh findeth; and to him that knocketh it shall be opened;" for only by patience, practice, and ceaseless importunity can a man enter the Door of the Temple of Knowledge.

EFFECT OF THOUGHT ON
CIRCUMSTANCES

MAN'S mind may be likened to a garden, which may be intelligently cultivated or allowed to run wild; but whether cultivated or neglected, it must, and will, *bring forth*. If no useful seeds are *put* into it, then an abundance of useless weed-seeds will *fall* therein, and will continue to produce their kind.

Just as a gardener cultivates his plot, keeping it free from weeds, and growing the flowers and fruits which he requires, so may a man tend the garden of his mind, weeding out all the wrong, useless, and impure thoughts, and cultivating toward perfection the flowers and fruits of right, useful, and pure thoughts. By pursuing this process, a man sooner or later discovers that he is the master-gardener of his soul, the director of his life. He also reveals, within himself, the laws of thought, and understands, with ever-increasing accuracy, how the thought-forces and mind elements operate in the shaping of his character, circumstances, and destiny.

Thought and character are one, and as character can only manifest and discover itself through environment and circumstance, the outer conditions of a person's life will always be found to be harmoniously related to his inner state. This does not mean that a man's circumstances at any given time are an indication of his *entire* character, but that those circumstances are so intimately connected with some vital thought-element within himself that, for the time being, they are indispensable to his development.

Every man is where he is by the law of his being; the thoughts which he has built into his character have brought him there, and in the arrangement of his life there is no element of chance, but all is the result of a law which cannot err. This is just as true of those who feel "out of harmony" with their surroundings as of those who are contented with them.

As a progressive and evolving being, man is where he is that he may learn that he may grow; and as he learns the spiritual lesson which any circumstance contains for him, it passes away and gives place to other circumstances.

Man is buffeted by circumstances so long as he believes himself to be the creature of outside conditions, but when he realizes that he is a creative power, and that he may command the hidden soil and seeds of his being out of which circumstances grow, he then becomes the rightful master of himself.

That circumstances grow out of thought every man knows who has for any length of time practised self-control and self-purification, for he will have noticed that the alteration in his circumstances has been in exact ratio with his altered mental condition. So true is this that when a man earnestly applies himself to

remedy the defects in his character, and makes swift
and marked progress, he passes rapidly through a suc-
cession of vicissitudes.

The soul attracts that which it secretly harbours; that
which it loves, and also that which it fears; it reaches the
height of its cherished aspirations; it falls to the level
of its unchastened desires,—and circumstances are the
means by which the soul receives its own.

Every thought-seed sown or allowed to fall into the
mind, and to take root there, produces its own, blossom-
ing sooner or later into act, and bearing its own fruitage of opportunity and circumstance. Good thoughts
bear good fruit, bad thoughts bad fruit.

The outer world of circumstance shapes itself to the
inner world of thought, and both pleasant and unpleas-
ant external conditions are factors, which make for the
ultimate good of the individual. As the reaper of his
own harvest, man learns both by suffering and bliss.

Following the inmost desires, aspirations, thoughts,
by which he allows himself to be dominated, (pursuing
the will-o'-the-wisps of impure imaginings or steadfastly walking the highway of strong and high endeav-
our), a man at last arrives at their fruition and fulfil-
ment in the outer conditions of his life. The laws of
growth and adjustment everywhere obtains.

A man does not come to the almshouse or the jail by
the tyranny of fate or circumstance, but by the pathway of grovelling thoughts and base desires. Nor does
a pure-minded man fall suddenly into crime by stress

of any mere external force; the criminal thought had long been secretly fostered in the heart, and the hour of opportunity revealed its gathered power. Circumstance does not make the man; it reveals him to himself No such conditions can exist as descending into vice and its attendant sufferings apart from vicious inclinations, or ascending into virtue and its pure happiness without the continued cultivation of virtuous aspirations; and man, therefore, as the lord and master of thought, is the maker of himself the shaper and author of environment. Even at birth the soul comes to its own and through every step of its earthly pilgrimage it attracts those combinations of conditions which reveal itself, which are the reflections of its own purity and, impurity, its strength and weakness.

Men do not attract that which they *want*, but that which they *are*. Their whims, fancies, and ambitions are thwarted at every step, but their inmost thoughts and desires are fed with their own food, be it foul or clean. The "divinity that shapes our ends" is in ourselves; it is our very self. Only himself manacles man: thought and action are the gaolers of Fate—they imprison, being base; they are also the angels of Freedom—they liberate, being noble. Not what he wishes and prays for does a man get, but what he justly earns. His wishes and prayers are only gratified and answered when they harmonize with his thoughts and actions.

In the light of this truth, what, then, is the meaning of "fighting against circumstances?" It means that a man is continually revolting against an *effect* without, while all the time he is nourishing and preserving its *cause* in his heart. That cause may take the form of a conscious vice or an unconscious weakness; but whatever it is, it stubbornly retards the efforts of its possessor, and thus calls aloud for remedy.

Men are anxious to improve their circumstances, but are unwilling to improve themselves; they therefore remain bound. The man who does not shrink from self-crucifixion can never fail to accomplish the object upon which his heart is set. This is as true of earthly as of heavenly things. Even the man whose sole object is to acquire wealth must be prepared to make great personal sacrifices before he can accomplish his object; and how much more so he who would realize a strong and well-poised life?

Here is a man who is wretchedly poor. He is extremely anxious that his surroundings and home comforts should be improved, yet all the time he shirks his work, and considers he is justified in trying to deceive his employer on the ground of the insufficiency of his wages. Such a man does not understand the simplest rudiments of those principles which are the basis of true prosperity, and is not only totally unfitted to rise out of his wretchedness, but is actually attracting to himself a still deeper wretchedness by dwelling in, and acting out, indolent, deceptive, and unmanly thoughts.

Here is a rich man who is the victim of a painful and persistent disease as the result of gluttony. He is willing to give large sums of money to get rid of it, but he will not sacrifice his gluttonous desires. He wants to gratify his taste for rich and unnatural viands and have his health as well. Such a man is totally unfit to have health, because he has not yet learned the first principles of a healthy life.

Here is an employer of labor who adopts crooked measures to avoid paying the regulation wage, and, in the hope of making larger profits, reduces the wages of his workpeople. Such a man is altogether unfitted for prosperity, and when he finds himself bankrupt, both as regards reputation and riches, he blames circumstances, not knowing that he is the sole author of his condition.

I have introduced these three cases merely as illustrative of the truth that man is the causer (though nearly always is unconsciously) of his circumstances, and that, whilst aiming at a good end, he is continually frustrating its accomplishment by encouraging thoughts and desires which cannot possibly harmonize with that end. Such cases could be multiplied and varied almost indefinitely, but this is not necessary, as the reader can, if he so resolves, trace the action of the laws of thought in his own mind and life, and until this is done, mere external facts cannot serve as a ground of reasoning.

Circumstances, however, are so complicated, thought is so deeply rooted, and the conditions of happiness vary so, vastly with individuals, that a man's entire soul-condition (although it may be known to himself) cannot be judged by another from the external aspect of his life alone. A man may be honest in certain directions, yet suffer privations; a man may be dishonest in certain directions, yet acquire wealth; but the conclusion usually formed that the one man fails *because of his particular honesty,* and that the other *prospers because of his particular dishonesty,* is the result of a superficial judgment, which assumes that the dishonest man is almost totally corrupt, and the honest man almost entirely virtuous. In the light of a deeper knowledge and wider experience such judgment is found to be erroneous. The dishonest man may have some admirable virtues, which the other does, not possess; and the honest man obnoxious vices which are absent in the other. The honest man reaps the good results of his honest thoughts and acts; he also brings upon himself the sufferings, which his vices produce. The dishonest man likewise garners his own suffering and happiness.

It is pleasing to human vanity to believe that one suffers because of one's virtue; but not until a man has extirpated every sickly, bitter, and impure thought from his mind, and washed every sinful stain from his soul, can he be in a position to know and declare that his sufferings are the result of his good, and not of his bad qualities; and on the way to, yet long before he has reached, that supreme perfection, he will have found, working in his mind and life, the Great Law which is absolutely just, and which cannot, therefore, give good for evil, evil for good. Possessed of such knowledge, he will then know, looking back upon his past ignorance and blindness, that his life is, and always was, justly ordered, and that all his past experiences, good and bad, were the equitable outworking of his evolving, yet unevolved self.

Good thoughts and actions can never produce bad results; bad thoughts and actions can never produce good results. This is but saying that nothing can come from corn but corn, nothing from nettles but nettles. Men understand this law in the natural world, and work with it; but few understand it in the mental and moral world (though its operation there is just as simple and undeviating), and they, therefore, do not co-operate with it.

Suffering is *always* the effect of wrong thought in some direction. It is an indication that the individual is out of harmony with himself, with the Law of his being. The sole and supreme use of suffering is to purify, to burn out all that is useless and impure. Suffering ceases for him who is pure. There could be no object in burning gold after the dross had been removed, and a perfectly pure and enlightened being could not suffer.

The circumstances, which a man encounters with suffering, are the result of his own mental in harmony. The circumstances, which a man encounters with blessedness, are the result of his own mental harmony. Blessedness, not material possessions, is the measure of right thought; wretchedness, not lack of material possessions, is the measure of wrong thought. A man may be cursed and rich; he may be blessed and poor.

Blessedness and riches are only joined together when the riches are rightly and wisely used; and the poor man only descends into wretchedness when he regards his lot as a burden unjustly imposed.

Indigence and indulgence are the two extremes of wretchedness. They are both equally unnatural and the result of mental disorder. A man is not rightly conditioned until he is a happy, healthy, and prosperous being; and happiness, health, and prosperity are the result of a harmonious adjustment of the inner with the outer, of the man with his surroundings.

A man only begins to be a man when he ceases to whine and revile, and commences to search for the hidden justice which regulates his life. And as he adapts his mind to that regulating factor, he ceases to accuse others as the cause of his condition, and builds himself up in strong and noble thoughts; ceases to kick against circumstances, but begins to *use* them as aids to his more rapid progress, and as a means of discovering the hidden powers and possibilities within himself.

Law, not confusion, is the dominating principle in the universe; justice, not injustice, is the soul and substance of life; and righteousness, not corruption, is the moulding and moving force in the spiritual government of the world. This being so, man has but to right himself to find that the universe is right; and during the process of putting himself right he will find that as he alters his thoughts towards things and other people, things and other people will alter towards him.

The proof of this truth is in every person, and it therefore admits of easy investigation by systematic introspection and self-analysis. Let a man radically alter his thoughts, and he will be astonished at the rapid transformation it will effect in the material conditions of his life. Men imagine that thought can be kept secret, but it cannot; it rapidly crystallizes into habit, and habit solidifies into circumstance. Bestial thoughts crystallize into habits of drunkenness and sensuality, which solidify into circumstances of destitution and disease: impure thoughts of every kind crystallize into enervating and confusing habits, which solidify into distracting and adverse circumstances: thoughts of fear, doubt, and indecision crystallize into weak, unmanly, and irresolute habits, which solidify into circumstances of failure, indigence, and slavish dependence: lazy thoughts crystallize into habits of uncleanliness and dishonesty, which solidify into circumstances of foulness and beggary: hateful and condemnatory thoughts crystallize into habits of accusation and violence, which solidify into circumstances of injury and persecution: selfish thoughts of all kinds crystallize into habits of self-seeking, which solidify into circumstances more or less distressing. On the other hand, beautiful thoughts of all kinds crystallize into habits of grace and kindliness, which solidify into genial and sunny circumstances: pure thoughts crystallize into habits of temperance and self-control, which solidify into circumstances of repose and peace: thoughts of courage, self-reliance, and decision crystallize into manly habits, which solidify into circumstances of success, plenty, and freedom: energetic thoughts crystallize into habits of cleanliness and industry, which solidify into circumstances of pleasantness: gentle and forgiving thoughts crystallize into habits of gentleness, which solidify into protective and preservative circumstances: loving and unselfish thoughts crystallize into habits of self-forgetfulness for others, which solidify into circumstances of sure and abiding prosperity and true riches.

A particular train of thought persisted in, be it good or bad, cannot fail to produce its results on the character and circumstances. A man cannot *directly* choose his circumstances, but he can choose his thoughts, and so indirectly, yet surely, shape his circumstances.

Nature helps every man to the gratification of the thoughts, which he most encourages, and opportunities are presented which will most speedily bring to the surface both the good and evil thoughts.

Let a man cease from his sinful thoughts, and all the world will soften towards him, and be ready to help him; let him put away his weakly and sickly thoughts, and lo, opportunities will spring up on every hand to aid his strong resolves; let him encourage good thoughts, and no hard fate shall bind him down to wretchedness and shame. The world is your kaleidoscope, and the varying combinations of colors, which at every succeeding moment it presents to you are the exquisitely adjusted pictures of your ever-moving thoughts.

"You will be what you will to be;
　　Let failure find its false content
　　In that poor word, 'environment,'
But spirit scorns it, and is free.

"It masters time, it conquers space;
　　It cowes that boastful trickster, Chance,
　　And bids the tyrant Circumstance
Uncrown, and fill a servant's place.

"The human Will, that force unseen,
　　The offspring of a deathless Soul,
　　Can hew a way to any goal,
Though walls of granite intervene.

"Be not impatient in delays
　　But wait as one who understands;
　　When spirit rises and commands
The gods are ready to obey."

EFFECT OF THOUGHT ON HEALTH
AND THE BODY

THE body is the servant of the mind. It obeys the operations of the mind, whether they be deliberately chosen or automatically expressed. At the bidding of unlawful thoughts the body sinks rapidly into disease and decay; at the command of glad and beautiful thoughts it becomes clothed with youthfulness and beauty.

Disease and health, like circumstances, are rooted in thought. Sickly thoughts will express themselves through a sickly body. Thoughts of fear have been known to kill a man as speedily as a bullet, and they are continually killing thousands of people just as surely though less rapidly. The people who live in fear of disease are the people who get it. Anxiety quickly demoralizes the whole body, and lays it open to the entrance of disease; while impure thoughts, even if not physically indulged, will soon shatter the nervous system.

Strong, pure, and happy thoughts build up the body in vigor and grace. The body is a delicate and plastic instrument, which responds readily to the thoughts by which it is impressed, and habits of thought will produce their own effects, good or bad, upon it.

Men will continue to have impure and poisoned blood, so long as they propagate unclean thoughts. Out of a clean heart comes a clean life and a clean body. Out of a defiled mind proceeds a defiled life and a corrupt body. Thought is the fount of action, life, and manifestation; make the fountain pure, and all will be pure.

Change of diet will not help a man who will not change his thoughts. When a man makes his thoughts pure, he no longer desires impure food.

Clean thoughts make clean habits. The so-called saint who does not wash his body is not a saint. He who has strengthened and purified his thoughts does not need to consider the malevolent microbe.

If you would protect your body, guard your mind. If you would renew your body, beautify your mind. Thoughts of malice, envy, disappointment, despondency, rob the body of its health and grace. A sour face does not come by chance; it is made by sour thoughts. Wrinkles that mar are drawn by folly, passion, and pride.

I know a woman of ninety-six who has the bright, innocent face of a girl. I know a man well under middle age whose face is drawn into inharmonious contours. The one is the result of a sweet and sunny disposition; the other is the outcome of passion and discontent.

As you cannot have a sweet and wholesome abode unless you admit the air and sunshine freely into your rooms, so a strong body and a bright, happy, or serene countenance can only result from the free admittance into the mind of thoughts of joy and goodwill and serenity.

On the faces of the aged there are wrinkles made by sympathy, others by strong and pure thought, and others are carved by passion: who cannot distinguish them? With those who have lived righteously, age is calm, peaceful, and softly mellowed, like the setting sun. I have recently seen a philosopher on his deathbed. He was not old except in years. He died as sweetly and peacefully as he had lived.

There is no physician like cheerful thought for dissipating the ills of the body; there is no comforter to compare with goodwill for dispersing the shadows of grief and sorrow. To live continually in thoughts of ill will, cynicism, suspicion, and envy, is to be confined in a self made prison-hole. But to think well of all, to be cheerful with all, to patiently learn to find the good in all—such unselfish thoughts are the very portals of heaven; and to dwell day by day in thoughts of peace toward every creature will bring abounding peace to their possessor.

THOUGHT AND PURPOSE

UNTIL thought is linked with purpose there is no intelligent accomplishment. With the majority the bark of thought is allowed to "drift" upon the ocean of life. Aimlessness is a vice, and such drifting must not continue for him who would steer clear of catastrophe and destruction.

They who have no central purpose in their life fall an easy prey to petty worries, fears, troubles, and self-pityings, all of which are indications of weakness, which lead, just as surely as deliberately planned sins (though by a different route), to failure, unhappiness, and loss, for weakness cannot persist in a power evolving universe.

A man should conceive of a legitimate purpose in his heart, and set out to accomplish it. He should make this purpose the centralizing point of his thoughts. It may take the form of a spiritual ideal, or it may be a worldly object, according to his nature at the time being; but whichever it is, he should steadily focus his thought-forces upon the object, which he has set before him. He should make this purpose his supreme duty, and should devote himself to its attainment, not allowing his thoughts to wander away into ephemeral fancies, longings, and imaginings. This is the royal road to self-control and true concentration of thought. Even if he fails again and again to accomplish his purpose (as he necessarily must until weakness is overcome), the *strength of character gained* will be the measure of *his true* success, and this will form a new starting-point for future power and triumph.

Those who are not prepared for the apprehension of a *great* purpose should fix the thoughts upon the faultless performance of their duty, no matter how insignificant their task may appear. Only in this way can the thoughts be gathered and focussed, and resolution and energy be developed, which being done, there is nothing which may not be accomplished.

The weakest soul, knowing its own weakness, and believing this truth *that strength can only be developed by effort and practice,* will, thus believing, at once begin to exert itself, and, adding effort to effort, patience to patience, and strength to strength, will never cease to develop, and will at last grow divinely strong.

As the physically weak man can make himself strong by careful and patient training, so the man of weak thoughts can make them strong by exercising himself in right thinking.

To put away aimlessness and weakness, and to begin to think with purpose, is to enter the ranks of those strong ones who only recognize failure as one of the pathways to attainment; who make all conditions serve them, and who think strongly, attempt fearlessly, and accomplish masterfully.

Having conceived of his purpose, a man should mentally mark out a *straight* pathway to its achievement, looking neither to the right nor the left. Doubts and fears should be rigorously excluded; they are disintegrating elements, which break up the straight line of effort, rendering it crooked, ineffectual, useless. Thoughts of doubt and fear never accomplished anything, and never can. They always lead to failure. Purpose, energy, power to do, and all strong thoughts cease when doubt and fear creep in.

The will to do springs from the knowledge that we *can* do. Doubt and fear are the great enemies of knowledge, and he who encourages them, who does not slay them, thwarts himself at every step.

He who has conquered doubt and fear has conquered failure. His every thought is allied with power, and all difficulties are bravely met and wisely overcome. His purposes are seasonably planted, and they bloom and bring forth fruit, which does not fall prematurely to the ground.

Thought allied fearlessly to purpose becomes creative force: he who *knows* this is ready to become something higher and stronger than a mere bundle of wavering thoughts and fluctuating sensations; he who *does* this has become the conscious and intelligent wielder of his mental powers.

THE THOUGHT-FACTOR IN
ACHIEVEMENT

ALL that a man achieves and all that he fails to
achieve is the direct result of his own thoughts. In
a justly ordered universe, where loss of equipoise would
mean total destruction, individual responsibility must
be absolute. A man's weakness and strength, purity and
impurity, are his own, and not another man's; they are
brought about by himself, and not by another; and they
can only be altered by himself, never by another. His
condition is also his own, and not another man's. His
suffering and his happiness are evolved from within.
As he thinks, so he is; as he continues to think, so he
remains.

A strong man cannot help a weaker unless that
weaker is *willing* to be helped, and even then the weak
man must become strong of himself; he must, by his
own efforts, develop the strength which he admires in
another. None but himself can alter his condition.

It has been usual for men to think and to say,
"Many men are slaves because one is an oppressor; let
us hate the oppressor." Now, however, there is amongst
an increasing few a tendency to reverse this judgment,
and to say, "One man is an oppressor because many are
slaves; let us despise the slaves."

The truth is that oppressor and slave are co-operators in ignorance, and, while seeming to afflict each other, are in reality afflicting themselves. A perfect Knowledge perceives the action of law in the weakness of the oppressed and the misapplied power of the oppressor; a perfect Love, seeing the suffering, which both states entail, condemns neither; a perfect Compassion embraces both oppressor and oppressed.

He who has conquered weakness, and has put away all selfish thoughts, belongs neither to oppressor nor oppressed. He is free.

A man can only rise, conquer, and achieve by lifting up his thoughts. He can only remain weak, and abject, and miserable by refusing to lift up his thoughts.

Before a man can achieve anything, even in worldly things, he must lift his thoughts above slavish animal indulgence. He may not, in order to succeed, give up all animality and selfishness, by any means; but a portion of it must, at least, be sacrificed. A man whose first thought is bestial indulgence could neither think clearly nor plan methodically; he could not find and develop his latent resources, and would fail in any undertaking. Not having commenced to manfully control his thoughts, he is not in a position to control affairs and to adopt serious responsibilities. He is not fit to act independently and stand alone. But he is limited only by the thoughts, which he chooses.

There can be no progress, no achievement without sacrifice, and a man's worldly success will be in the measure that he sacrifices his confused animal thoughts, and fixes his mind on the development of his plans, and the strengthening of his resolution and self-reliance. And the higher he lifts his thoughts, the more manly, upright, and righteous he becomes, the greater will be his success, the more blessed and enduring will be his achievements.

The universe does not favor the greedy, the dishonest, the vicious, although on the mere surface it may sometimes appear to do so; it helps the honest, the magnanimous, the virtuous. All the great Teachers of the ages have declared this in varying forms, and to prove and know it a man has but to persist in making himself more and more virtuous by lifting up his thoughts.

Intellectual achievements are the result of thought consecrated to the search for knowledge, or for the beautiful and true in life and nature. Such achievements may be sometimes connected with vanity and ambition, but they are not the outcome of those characteristics; they are the natural outgrowth of long and arduous effort, and of pure and unselfish thoughts.

Spiritual achievements are the consummation of holy aspirations. He who lives constantly in the conception of noble and lofty thoughts, who dwells upon all that is pure and unselfish, will, as surely as the sun reaches its zenith and the moon its full, become wise and noble in character, and rise into a position of influence and blessedness.

Achievement, of whatever kind, is the crown of effort, the diadem of thought. By the aid of self-control, resolution, purity, righteousness, and well-directed thought a man ascends; by the aid of animality, indolence, impurity, corruption, and confusion of thought a man descends.

A man may rise to high success in the world, and even to lofty altitudes in the spiritual realm, and again descend into weakness and wretchedness by allowing arrogant, selfish, and corrupt thoughts to take possession of him.

Victories attained by right thought can only be maintained by watchfulness. Many give way when success is assured, and rapidly fall back into failure.

All achievements, whether in the business, intellectual, or spiritual world, are the result of definitely directed thought, are governed by the same law and are of the same method; the only difference lies in *the object of attainment*.

He who would accomplish little must sacrifice little; he who would achieve much must sacrifice much; he who would attain highly must sacrifice greatly.

VISIONS AND IDEALS

THE dreamers are the saviours of the world. As the visible world is sustained by the invisible, so men, through all their trials and sins and sordid vocations, are nourished by the beautiful visions of their solitary dreamers. Humanity cannot forget its dreamers; it cannot let their ideals fade and die; it lives in them; it knows them as the *realities* which it shall one day see and know.

Composer, sculptor, painter, poet, prophet, sage, these are the makers of the after-world, the architects of heaven. The world is beautiful because they have lived; without them, labouring humanity would perish.

He who cherishes a beautiful vision, a lofty ideal in his heart, will one day realize it. Columbus cherished a vision of another world, and he discovered it; Copernicus fostered the vision of a multiplicity of worlds and a wider universe, and he revealed it; Buddha beheld the vision of a spiritual world of stainless beauty and perfect peace, and he entered into it.

Cherish your visions; cherish your ideals; cherish the music that stirs in your heart, the beauty that forms in your mind, the loveliness that drapes your purest thoughts, for out of them will grow all delightful conditions, all, heavenly environment; of these, if you but remain true to them, your world will at last be built.

To desire is to obtain; to aspire is to, achieve. Shall man's basest desires receive the fullest measure of gratification, and his purest aspirations starve for lack of sustenance? Such is not the Law: such a condition of things can never obtain: "ask and receive."

Dream lofty dreams, and as you dream, so shall you become. Your Vision is the promise of what you shall one day be; your Ideal is the prophecy of what you shall at last unveil.

The greatest achievement was at first and for a time a dream. The oak sleeps in the acorn; the bird waits in the egg; and in the highest vision of the soul a waking angel stirs. Dreams are the seedlings of realities.

Your circumstances may be uncongenial, but they shall not long remain so if you but perceive an Ideal and strive to reach it. You cannot travel *within* and stand still *without*. Here is a youth hard pressed by poverty and labor; confined long hours in an unhealthy workshop; unschooled, and lacking all the arts of refinement. But he dreams of better things; he thinks of intelligence, of refinement, of grace and beauty. He conceives of, mentally builds up, an ideal condition of life; the vision of a wider liberty and a larger scope takes possession of him; unrest urges him to action, and he utilizes all his spare time and means, small though they are, to the development of his latent powers and resources. Very soon so altered has his mind become that the workshop can no longer hold him. It has become so out of harmony with his mentality that it falls out of his life as a

garment is cast aside, and, with the growth of opportunities, which fit the scope of his expanding powers,
he passes out of it forever. Years later we see this youth
as a full-grown man. We find him a master of certain
forces of the mind, which he wields with worldwide influence and almost unequalled power. In his hands he
holds the cords of gigantic responsibilities; he speaks,
and lo, lives are changed; men and women hang upon
his words and remold their characters, and, sunlike, he
becomes the fixed and luminous centre round which innumerable destinies revolve. He has realized the Vision
of his youth. He has become one with his Ideal.

And you, too, youthful reader, will realize the Vision (not the idle wish) of your heart, be it base or beautiful, or a mixture of both, for you will always gravi-
tate toward that which you, secretly, most love. Into
your hands will be placed the exact results of your own
thoughts; you will receive that which you earn; no more,
no less. Whatever your present environment may be,
you will fall, remain, or rise with your thoughts, your
Vision, your Ideal. You will become as small as your
controlling desire; as great as your dominant aspiration: in the beautiful words of Stanton Kirkham Davis,
"You may be keeping accounts, and presently you shall
walk out of the door that for so long has seemed to you
the barrier of your ideals, and shall find yourself before an audience—the pen still behind your ear, the ink
stains on your fingers and then and there shall pour
out the torrent of your inspiration. You may be driving sheep, and you shall wander to the city-bucolic and

open-mouthed; shall wander under the intrepid guidance of the spirit into the studio of the master, and after a time he shall say, 'I have nothing more to teach you.' And now you have become the master, who did so recently dream of great things while driving sheep. You shall lay down the saw and the plane to take upon yourself the regeneration of the world."

The thoughtless, the ignorant, and the indolent, seeing only the apparent effects of things and not the things themselves, talk of luck, of fortune, and chance. Seeing a man grow rich, they say, "How lucky he is!" Observing another become intellectual, they exclaim, "How highly favoured he is!" And noting the saintly character and wide influence of another, they remark, "How chance aids him at every turn!" They do not see the trials and failures and struggles which these men have voluntarily encountered in order to gain their experience; have no knowledge of the sacrifices they have made, of the undaunted efforts they have put forth, of the faith they have exercised, that they might overcome the apparently insurmountable, and realize the Vision of their heart. They do not know the darkness and the heartaches; they only see the light and joy, and call it "luck". They do not see the long and arduous journey, but only behold the pleasant goal, and call it "good fortune," do not understand the process, but only perceive the result, and call it chance.

In all human affairs there are *efforts,* and there are *results,* and the strength of the effort is the measure of the result. Chance is not. Gifts, powers, material, intellectual, and spiritual possessions are the fruits of effort; they are thoughts completed, objects accomplished, visions realized.

The Vision that you glorify in your mind, the Ideal that you enthrone in your heart—this you will build your life by, this you will become.

SERENITY

CALMNESS of mind is one of the beautiful jewels of wisdom. It is the result of long and patient effort in self-control. Its presence is an indication of ripened experience, and of a more than ordinary knowledge of the laws and operations of thought.

A man becomes calm in the measure that he understands himself as a thought evolved being, for such knowledge necessitates the understanding of others as the result of thought, and as he develops a right understanding, and sees more and more clearly the internal relations of things by the action of cause and effect he ceases to fuss and fume and worry and grieve, and remains poised, steadfast, serene.

The calm man, having learned how to govern himself, knows how to adapt himself to others; and they, in turn, reverence his spiritual strength, and feel that they can learn of him and rely upon him. The more tranquil a man becomes, the greater is his success, his influence, his power for good. Even the ordinary trader will find his business prosperity increase as he develops a greater self-control and equanimity, for people will always prefer to deal with a man whose demeanor is strongly equable.

The strong, calm man is always loved and revered. He is like a shade-giving tree in a thirsty land, or a sheltering rock in a storm. "Who does not love a tranquil heart, a sweet-tempered, balanced life? It does not matter whether it rains or shines, or what changes come to those possessing these blessings, for they are always sweet, serene, and calm. That exquisite poise of character, which we call serenity is the last lesson of culture, the fruitage of the soul. It is precious as wisdom, more to be desired than gold—yea, than even fine gold. How insignificant mere money seeking looks in comparison with a serene life—a life that dwells in the ocean of Truth, beneath the waves, beyond the reach of tempests, in the Eternal Calm!

"How many people we know who sour their lives, who ruin all that is sweet and beautiful by explosive tempers, who destroy their poise of character, and make bad blood! It is a question whether the great majority of people do not ruin their lives and mar their happiness by lack of self-control. How few people we meet in life who are well balanced, who have that exquisite poise which is characteristic of the finished character!

Yes, humanity surges with uncontrolled passion, is tumultuous with ungoverned grief, is blown about by anxiety and doubt only the wise man, only he whose thoughts are controlled and purified, makes the winds and the storms of the soul obey him.

Tempest-tossed souls, wherever ye may be, under whatsoever conditions ye may live, know this in the ocean of life the isles of Blessedness are smiling, and the sunny shore of your ideal awaits your coming. Keep your hand firmly upon the helm of thought. In the bark of your soul reclines the commanding Master; He does but sleep: wake Him. Self-control is strength; Right Thought is mastery; Calmness is power. Say unto your heart, "Peace, be still!"

Out from the Heart

Make pure thy heart, and thou wilt make thy life
Rich, sweet, and beautiful, unmarred by strife;
Guard well thy mind, and, noble, strong, and free,
Nothing shall harm, disturb, or conquer thee;
For all thy foes are in thy heart and mind,
There also thy salvation thou wilt find.

FOREWORD

CONFUCIUS said, "The perfecting of one's self
is the fundamental base of all progress and all
moral development"; a maxim as profound and
comprehensive as it is simple , practical and uninvolved, for there is no surer way to knowledge,
nor no better way to help the world than by perfecting one's self. Nor is there any nobler work
or higher science than that of self-perfection. He
who studies how to become faultless, who strives
to be pure hearted, who aims at the possession of
a calm, wise, and seeing mind, engages in the
most sublime task that man can undertake, and
the results of which are perceptible in a well-ordered, blessed and beautiful life.

JAMES ALLEN

BROAD PARK AVENUE,
    ILFRACOMBE,
        ENGLAND.

OUT FROM THE HEART

THE HEART AND THE LIFE

AS THE HEART, SO IS THE LIFE. The within IS ceaselessly becoming the without. Nothing remains unrevealed. That which is hidden is but for a time; it ripens and comes forth at last. Seed, tree, blossom, and fruit are the fourfold order of the universe. From the state of a man's heart proceed the conditions of his life. His thoughts blossom into deeds; and his deeds bear the fruitage of character and destiny.

Life is ever unfolding from within, and revealing itself to the light, and thoughts engendered in the heart at last reveal themselves in words, actions, and things accomplished.

As the fountain from the hidden spring, so flows forth a man's life from the secret recesses of his heart. All that he is and does is generated there. All that he will be and do will take its rise there.

Sorrow and happiness, suffering and enjoyment, fear and hope, hatred and love, ignorance and enlightenment, are nowhere but in the heart. They are solely mental conditions.

Man is the keeper of his heart; the watcher of his mind; the solitary guard of his citadel of life. As such, he can be diligent or negligent. He can keep his heart more and more carefully. He can more strenuously watch and purify his mind; and he can guard against the thinking of unrighteous thoughts—this is the way of enlightenment and bliss.

On the other hand, he can live loosely and carelessly, neglecting the supreme task of rightfully ordering his life—this is the way of self-delusion and suffering.

Let a man realize that life in its totality proceeds from the mind, and lo, the way of blessedness is opened up to him! For he will then discover that he possesses the power to rule his mind, and to fashion it in accordance with his Ideal. So will he elect to strongly and steadfastly walk those pathways of thought and action which are altogether excellent. To him, life will become beautiful and sacred; and sooner or later, he will put to flight all evil, confusion, and suffering. For it is impossible for a man to fall short of liberation, enlightenment, and peace, who guards with unwearying diligence the gateway of his heart.

THE NATURE AND POWER OF MIND

MIND IS THE ARBITER of life. It is the creator and shaper of conditions, and the recipient of its own results. It contains within itself both the power to create illusion and to perceive reality. Mind is the infallible weaver of destiny. Thought is the thread, good and evil deeds are the "warp and woof" or foundation, and the web, woven upon the loom of life, is character. Mind clothes itself in garments of its own making.

Man, as a mental being, possesses all the powers of mind, and is furnished with unlimited choice. He learns by experience, and he can accelerate or retard his experience. He is not arbitrarily bound at any point, but he has bound himself at many points, and having bound himself he can, when he chooses, liberate himself.

He can become bestial or pure, ignorant or noble, foolish or wise, just as he chooses. He can, by reoccurring practice, form habits, and he can, by renewed effort, break them off. He can surround himself with illusions until Truth is completely lost, and he can destroy each of those illusions until Truth is entirely recovered. His possibilities are endless; his freedom is complete.

It is the nature of the mind to create its own conditions, and to choose the states in which it shall dwell. It also has the power to alter any condition, to abandon any state. This it is continually doing as it gathers knowledge of state after state by repeated choice and exhaustive experience.

Inward processes of thought make up the sum of character and life. Man can modify and alter these processes by bringing will and effort to bear upon them. The bonds of habit, impotence, and sin are self-made, and can only be destroyed by one's self. They exist nowhere but in one's mind, and although they are directly related to outward things, they have no real existence in those things.

The outer is molded and animated by the inner, and never the inner by the outer. Temptation does not arise in the outer object, but *in the lust of the mind for that object.* Nor do sorrow and suffering belong by nature to the external things and happenings of life, but in an undisciplined attitude of mind toward those things and happenings.

The mind that is disciplined by Purity and fortified by Wisdom avoids all those lusts and desires which are inseparately bound up with affliction, and so arrives at enlightenment and peace.

To condemn others as evil, and to curse at outside conditions as the source of evil, increases and does not lessen, the world's suffering and unrest. The outer is but the shadow and effect of the inner, and when the heart is pure all outward things are pure.

All growth and life is from within outward; all decay and death is from without inward. This is the universal law. All evolution proceeds from within. All adjustment must take place within. He who ceases to strive against others, and employs his powers in the transformation, regeneration, and development of his own mind, conserves his energies and preserves himself. And as he succeeds in harmonizing his own mind, he leads others by consideration and charity into a like blessed state.

The way of enlightenment and peace is not gained by assuming authority and guidance over other minds, but by exercising a lawful authority over one's own mind, and by guiding one's self in pathways of steadfast and lofty virtue.

A man's life proceeds from his heart and his mind. He has compounded that mind by his own thoughts and deeds. It is within his power to refashion that mind by his choice of thought. In this manner he can transform his life. Let us see how this is to be done.

FORMATION OF HABIT

EVERY ESTABLISHED mental condition is an *acquired habit*, and it has become such by continuous repetition of thought. Despondency and cheerfulness, anger and calmness, covetousness and generosity—indeed, all states of mind—are habits built up by choice, until they have become automatic. A thought constantly repeated at last becomes a fixed habit of the mind, and from such habits proceeds one's life.

It is in the nature of the mind to acquire knowledge by the repetition of its experiences. A thought which is very difficult, at first, to hold and dwell upon, at last becomes, by constantly being held in the mind, a natural and habitual practice.

A boy, when commencing to learn a trade, cannot even handle his tools right, much less use them correctly, but after long repetition and practice, he plies them with perfect ease and consummate skill. Likewise, a state of mind, at first apparently incapable of realization, is, by perseverance and practice, at last acquired and built into the character as a natural and spontaneous condition.

In this power of the mind to form and reform its habits, its conditions, is contained the basis of a man's salvation. It is the open door to perfect liberty by the mastery of self. For as a man has the power to form harmful habits, so he equally has the same power to create habits that are essentially good. And here we come to a point which needs some clarifying, and which calls for deep and earnest thought on the part of my reader.

It is commonly said to be easier to do wrong than right, to sin than to be holy. Such a condition has come to be regarded, almost universally, as a self-evident truth.

No less a teacher than the Buddha has said: "Bad deeds, and deeds hurtful to ourselves, are easy to do; what is beneficial and good, that is very difficult to do."

And with regards to humanity generally, this is true, but it is only true as a passing experience, a fleeting factor in human evolution. It is not a fixed condition of things. It is not the nature of an eternal truth. It is easier for men to do wrong than right, because of the prevalence of *ignorance*, because the true nature of things, and the essence and meaning of life, are not understood.

When a child is learning to write, it is extremely easy to hold the pen wrongly, and to form his letters incorrectly, but it is painfully difficult to hold the pen and to write properly. This is because of the child's ignorance of the art of writing, which can only be dispelled by persistent effort and practice, until, at last, it becomes natural and easy to hold the pen correctly, and difficult, as well as altogether unnecessary, to do the wrong thing.

It is the same in the vital things of mind and life. To think and do rightly requires much practice and renewed effort. But the time comes at last when it becomes habitual and easy to think and do rightly, and difficult, as it is then seen to be altogether unnecessary, to do that which is wrong.

Just as an artisan becomes, by practice, accomplished in his craft, so you can become, by practice, accomplished in goodness. It is entirely a matter of forming new habits of thought. And he to whom right thoughts have become easy and natural, and wrong thoughts and acts difficult to do, has attained to the highest virtue, to pure spiritual knowledge.

It is easy and natural for men to sin because they have formed by incessant repetition, harmful and unenlightened habits of thought. It is very difficult for the thief to refrain from stealing when the opportunity occurs, because he has lived so long in covetous and greedy thoughts.

But such difficulty does not exist for the honest man who has lived so long with upright and honest thoughts. He has thereby become so enlightened as to the wrong, folly, and fruitlessness of theft, that even the remotest idea of stealing does not enter his mind. The sin of theft is a very extreme one, and I have introduced it in order to more clearly illustrate the force and formation of habit. But all sins and virtues are formed in the same way.

Anger and impatience are natural and easy to thousands of people, because they are constantly repeating angry and impatient thoughts and acts. And with each repetition the habit is more firmly established and more deeply rooted.

Calmness and patience can become habitual in the same way—by first grasping through effort, a calm and patient thought, and then continuously thinking it, and living in it, until "use becomes second nature," and anger and impatience pass away forever. It is in this manner that every wrong thought may be expelled from the mind; that every untrue act may be destroyed; that every sin may be overcome.

DOING AND KNOWING

LET A MAN REALIZE that his life, in its totality, proceeds from his mind. Let him realize that
the mind is a combination of habits which he can, by
patient effort, modify to any extent, and over which he
can thus gain complete ascendancy, mastery, and control. At once, he will have obtained possession of the key
which shall open the door to his complete emancipation.

But freedom from the ills of life (which are the ills
of one's mind) is a matter of steady growth from within, and not a sudden acquisition from without. Hourly
and daily must the mind be trained to think stainless
thoughts, and adapt right and dispassionate attitudes
under those circumstances in which it is prone to fall
into wrong and passion. Like the patient sculptor upon
his marble, the aspirant to the Right Life must gradually work upon the crude material of his mind until he
has wrought out of it the Ideal of his holiest dreams.

In working toward such supreme accomplishment,
it is necessary to begin at the lowest and easiest steps,
and proceed by natural, progressive stages to the higher
and more difficult. This law of growth, progress, evolution, and unfoldment, by gradual and ever ascending
stages, is absolute in every department of life, and in
every human accomplishment. Where it is ignored, total failure will result.

In acquiring education, in learning a trade, or in pursuing a business, this law is fully recognized and minutely obeyed by all. But in acquiring Virtue, in learning Truth, and in pursuing the right conduct and knowledge of life, it is unrecognized and disobeyed by nearly all. Hence Virtue, Truth, and the Perfect Life remain unpracticed, unacquired, and unknown.

It is a common error to suppose that the Higher Life is a matter of reading, and the adoption of theological or metaphysical hypotheses, and that Spiritual Principles can be understood by this method. The Higher Life is *higher living* in thought, word, and deed, and the knowledge of those Spiritual Principles which are imminent in man and in the universe can only be acquired after long discipline in the pursuit and practice of Virtue.

The lesser must be thoroughly grasped and understood before the greater can be known. Practice always precedes *real* knowledge.

The schoolmaster never attempts to teach his pupils the abstract principles of mathematics at the start. He knows that such a method of teaching would be in vain, and learning impossible. He first places before them a simple sum, and, having explained it, leaves them to *do it*. When, after repeated failures and ever renewed effort, they have succeeded in doing it correctly, a more difficult task is set before them, and then another and another. It is not until the pupils have, through many years of diligent application, mastered all the lessons in arithmetic, that he attempts to unfold to them the underlying mathematical principles.

In learning a trade, say that of a mechanic, a boy is not at first taught the principles of mechanics, but a simple tool is put in his hand and he is told how rightly to use it. He is then left to do it by effort and practice. As he succeeds in plying his tools correctly, more and more difficult tasks are set before him, until after several years of successful practice, he is prepared to study and grasp the principles of mechanics.

In a properly governed household, the child is first taught to be obedient, and to conduct himself properly under all circumstances. The child is not even told why he must do this, but is commanded to do it. Only after he has far succeeded in doing what is right and proper, is he told *why* he should do it. No father would attempt to teach his child the principles of ethics before exacting from him the practice of family duty and social virtue.

Thus practice ever precedes knowledge even in the ordinary things of the world, and in spiritual things, in the living of the Higher Life, this law is rigid in its demands.

Virtue can only be known by *doing*, and the knowledge of Truth can only be arrived at by perfecting oneself in the practice of Virtue. To be complete in the practice and acquisition of Virtue is to be complete in the knowledge of Truth.

Truth can only be arrived at by daily and hourly doing the lessons of Virtue, beginning with the simplest, and passing on to the more difficult. A child patiently and obediently learns his lessons at school by constantly practicing, ever exerting himself until all failures and difficulties are surmounted. Likewise does the child of Truth, undaunted by failure, and made stronger by difficulties, apply himself to right doing in thought and action. As he succeeds in acquiring Virtue, his mind unfolds itself in the knowledge of Truth, and it is a knowledge in which he can securely rest.

FIRST STEPS IN THE HIGHER LIFE

SEEING THAT THE PATH OF VIRTUE is the Path of Knowledge, and that before the all-embracing Principles of Truth can be comprehended, perfection in the more lowly steps must be acquired, how, then, shall a disciple of Truth begin?

How shall one who aspires to the righting of his mind and the purification of his heart— that heart which is the fountain and repository of all the issues of life—learn the lessons of Virtue? How does he thus build himself up in the strength of knowledge, destroying ignorance and the ills of life? What are the first lessons, the first steps? How are they learned? How are they practiced? How are they mastered and understood?

The first lessons consist in overcoming those wrong mental conditions which are most easily eradicated, and which are the common barriers to spiritual progress, as well as in practicing the simple domestic and social virtues. The reader will be better aided if I group and classify the first ten steps in three lessons as follows:

VICES OF THE BODY TO BE OVERCOME AND ERADICATED

VICES OF THE BODY

(*First Lesson*: Discipline of the Body)

1: Idleness, Laziness or Indolence

2: Self-Indulgence or Gluttony

VICES OF THE TONGUE

(*Second Lesson*: Discipline of Speech)

1: Slander

2: Gossip and Idle Conversation

3: Abusive and Unkind Speech

4: Frivolity or Irreverent Speech

5: Critical, Captious or Fault-finding Speech

VIRTUES TO BE PRACTISED AND ACQUIRED

(*Third Lesson*: Discipline of Inclination)

1: Unselfish Performance of Duty

2: Unswerving Rectitude or Moral Integrity

3: Unlimited Forgiveness

The two vices of the body, and the five of the tongue, are so called because they are manifested in the body and tongue. Also, by so definitely classifying them, the mind of the reader will be better helped. But it must be clearly understood that these vices arise primarily in the mind, and are wrong conditions of the heart worked out in the body and the tongue.

The existence of such chaotic conditions is an indication that the mind is altogether unenlightened as to the real meaning and purpose of life, and their eradication is the beginning of a virtuous, steadfast, and enlightened life.

But how shall these vices be overcome and eradicated? By first, and at once, checking and controlling their outward manifestations and by suppressing the wrong act. This will stimulate the mind to watchfulness and reflection until, by repeated practice, it will come to perceive and understand the dark, wrong, and erroneous conditions of mind, out of which such acts spring. It will then abandon them entirely.

It will be seen that the first step in the discipline of the mind is the overcoming of indolence or laziness. This is the easiest step, and until it is perfectly accomplished, the other steps cannot be taken. The clinging to indolence constitutes a complete barrier to the Path of Truth. Indolence consists in giving the body more ease and sleep than it requires, in procrastinating, and in shirking and neglecting those things which should receive immediate attention.

This condition of laziness must be overcome by rousing up the body at an early hour, giving it just the amount of sleep it requires for complete recuperation, and by doing promptly and vigorously, every task, every duty, no matter how small, as it comes along.

On no account should food or drink be taken in bed. And to lie in bed after one has awakened, indulging in ease and reverie, is a habit fatal to promptness and resolution of character, and purity of mind. Nor should one attempt to do his thinking at such a time. Strong, pure, and true thinking is impossible under such circumstances. A man should go to bed to sleep, not to think. He should get up to think and work, not to sleep.

The next step is the overcoming of self-indulgence or gluttony. The glutton is he who eats for animal gratification only, without considering the true end and object of eating. He eats more than his body requires, and is greedy after sweet things and rich dishes.

Such undisciplined desire can only be overcome by reducing the quantity of food eaten, and the number of meals per day, and by resorting to a simple and uninvolved diet. Regular hours should be set apart for meals, and eating at other times should be rigidly avoided. Suppers should be abolished, as they are altogether unnecessary, and promote heavy sleep and cloudiness of mind.

The pursuit of such a method of discipline will rapidly bring the once ungoverned appetite under control, and as the sensual sin of self-indulgence is taken out of the mind, the right selection of foods will be instinctively and infallibly adapted to the purified mental condition.

It should be well borne in mind that a *change of heart* is the needful thing, and that any change of diet which does not promote this end is futile. When one eats for enjoyment, he is gluttonous. The heart must be purified of sensual craving and gustatory lust.

When the body is well controlled and firmly guided; when that which is to be done is done vigorously;

when no task or duty is delayed; when early rising has become a delight; when frugality, simplicity, temperance, and abstinence are firmly established; when one is contented with the food which is put before him, no matter how scanty and plain, and the craving for gustatory pleasure is at an end—then the first two steps in the Higher Life are accomplished. Then is the first great lesson in Truth learned. Thus is established in the heart the foundation of a poised, self-governed, virtuous life.

The next lesson is the lesson of Virtuous Speech, in which there are five orderly steps.

The first of these is overcoming the habit of slanderous speech. Slander consists of inventing or repeating unkind and evil reports about others, in exposing and magnifying the faults of others, or of absent friends, and in introducing unworthy insinuations. The elements of thoughtlessness, cruelty, insincerity, and untruthfulness enter into every slanderous act.

He who aims at the living of the right life will commence to check the cruel word of slander before it has gone forth from his lips. He will then check and eliminate the insincere thought which gave rise to it.

He will watch that he does not vilify or defame anyone. He will refrain from disparaging, defaming, and condemning the absent friend, whose face he has so recently smiled into or kissed, or whose hand he has shaken. He will not say *of* another that which he dare not say *to* his face. Thus, coming at last to think sacredly of the character and reputation of others, he will destroy those wrong conditions of mind which give rise to slander.

The next step is the overcoming of gossip and idle conversation. Idle speech consists in talking about the private affairs of others, in talking merely to pass away the time, and in engaging in aimless and irrelevant conversation. Such an ungoverned condition of speech is the outcome of an ill-regulated mind.

The man of virtue will bridle his tongue, and thus learn how rightly to govern the mind. He will not let his tongue run idly and foolishly, but will make his speech strong and pure, and will either talk with a purpose or remain silent.

Abusive and unkind speech is the next vice to be overcome. The man who abuses and accuses others has himself wandered far from the Right Way. To hurl hard words and names at others is to sink deeply into folly. When a man is inclined to abuse, curse, and condemn others, let him restrain his tongue and look within himself. The virtuous man refrains from all abusive language and quarrelling. He employs only words that are useful, necessary, pure, and true.

The sixth step is the overcoming of levity, or irreverent speech. Light and frivolous talking; the repeating of crude jokes; the telling of vulgar stories, having no other purpose than to raise an empty laugh; offensive familiarity, and the employment of contemptuous and disrespectful words when speaking to or of others, and particularly of one's elders and those who rank as one's teachers, guardians or superiors—all of this will he put away by the lover of Virtue and Truth.

Upon the altar of irreverence absent friends and companions are immolated for the passing excitement of a momentary laugh, and all the sanctity of life is sacrificed to the zest for ridicule. When respect towards others and the giving of reverence where reverence is due are abandoned, Virtue is abandoned. When modesty, significance, and dignity are eliminated from speech and behavior, Truth is lost. Yea, even its entrance gate is hidden away and forgotten.

Irreverence is degrading even in the young, but when it accompanies grey hairs, and appears in the demeanor of the preacher—this is indeed a piteous spectacle. And when this can be imitated and followed after, then are the blind leading the blind, then have elders, preachers, and people lost their way.

The virtuous will be of earnest and reverent speech. He will think and speak of the absent as he thinks and speaks of the dead—tenderly and sacredly. He will put away thoughtlessness, and watch that he does not sacrifice his dignity to gratify a passing impulse to frivolity and superficiality. His humor will be pure and innocent, his voice will be subdued and musical, and his soul will be filled with grace and sweetness as he succeeds in conducting himself as becomes a man of Truth.

The last step in the second lesson is the overcoming of criticism, or fault-finding speech. This vice of the tongue consists in magnifying and harping on small or apparent faults, in foolish quibbling and hair-splitting, and in pursuing vain arguments based upon groundless suppositions, beliefs, and opinions.

Life is short and real, and sin, sorrow and pain are not remedied by carping and contention. The man who is ever on the watch to catch at the words of others in order to contradict and dispute them, has yet to reach the higher way of holiness, the truer life of self-surrender. The man who is ever on the alert to check his own words in order to soften and purify them will find the higher way and the truer life. He will conserve his energies, maintain his composure of mind, and preserve within himself the spirit of Truth.

When the tongue is well controlled and wisely subdued; when selfish impulses and unworthy thoughts no longer rush to the tongue demanding utterance; when the speech has become harmless, pure, gentle, gracious, and purposeful, and no word is uttered but in sincerity and honesty—then are the five steps to virtuous speech accomplished, then is the second great lesson in Truth learned and mastered.

And now some will ask, "But why all this discipline of the body and restraint of the tongue? Surely the Higher Life can be realized and known without such strenuous labor, such incessant effort and watchfulness?" No, it cannot. In the spiritual as the material, nothing is done without labor, and the higher cannot be known until the lower is fulfilled.

Can a man make a table before he has learned how to handle a tool and drive a nail? And can a man fashion his mind in accordance with Truth before he has overcome the slavery of his body?

As the intricate subtleties of language cannot be understood and wielded before the alphabet and the simplest words are mastered, neither can the deep subtleties of the mind be understood and purified before the ABC of right conduct is perfectly acquired.

As for the labor involved—does not the youth joyfully and patiently submit himself to a seven-years' apprenticeship in order to master a craft? And does he not, day by day, carefully and faithfully carry out every detail of his master's instructions, looking forward to the time when, perfected through obedience and practice, he shall be himself a master?

Where is the man who sincerely aims at excellence in music, painting, literature, or in any trade, business, or profession who is not willing to give his whole life to the acquirement of that particular perfection? Shall labor, then, be considered where the very highest excellence is concerned—the excellence of Truth?

He who says, "The Path which you have pointed out is too difficult; I must have Truth without labor, salvation without effort," that man will not find his way out of the confusions and sufferings of selfhood. He will not find the calm, well-fortified mind and the wisely ordered life. His love is for ease and enjoyment, and not for Truth.

He who, deep in his heart, adores Truth, and aspires to know it, will consider no labor too great to be undertaken, but will adopt it joyfully and pursue it patiently. By perseverance in practice he will come to the knowledge of Truth.

The necessity for this preliminary discipline of the body and tongue will be more clearly perceived when it is fully understood that all these wrong outward conditions are merely the expressions of wrong conditions of the heart. An indolent body means an indolent mind; an ill-regulated tongue reveals an ill-regulated mind, and the process of remedying the manifested condition is really a method of rectifying the inward state.

Moreover, the overcoming of these conditions is only a small part of what is really involved in the process. The ceasing from evil leads to, and is inseparably connected with, the practice of good. While a man is overcoming laziness and self-indulgence, he is really cultivating and developing the virtues of abstinence, temperance, punctuality, and self-denial. He is acquiring the strength, energy, and resolve which are indispensable to the successful accomplishment of the higher tasks. While he is overcoming the vices of speech, he is developing the virtues of truthfulness, sincerity, reverence, kindliness, and self-control, and is gaining that mental steadiness and fixedness of purpose, without which the more remote subtleties of the mind cannot be regulated, and the higher stages of conduct and enlightenment cannot be reached.

Also, as he learns to *do* right, his knowledge deepens, and his insight is intensified. Just as a child's heart is glad when a school task is mastered, so with each victory achieved, the man of virtue experiences a bliss which the seeker after pleas ure and excitement can never know.

And now we come to the third lesson in the Higher Life, which consists of practicing and mastering, in one's daily life, three great fundamental Virtues:

1) Unselfish Performance of Duty

2) Unswerving Rectitude (Moral Integrity)

3) Unlimited Forgiveness

Having prepared the mind by overcoming the more surface and chaotic conditions mentioned in the first two lessons, the striver after Virtue and Truth is now ready to enter upon greater and more difficult tasks, and to control and purify the deeper motives of the heart.

Without the right performance of duty, the higher virtues cannot be known, and Truth cannot be apprehended. Duty is generally regarded as an irksome labor, a compulsory something which must be toiled through, or be in some way avoided. This way of regarding duty proceeds from a selfish condition of mind, and a wrong understanding of life. All duty should be regarded as sacred, and it s faithful and unselfish performance one of the leading rules of conduct. All personal and selfish considerations should be extracted and cast away from the doing of one's duty, and when this is done, duty ceases to be irksome, and becomes joyful. Duty is only irksome to him who craves some selfish enjoyment or benefit for himself. Let the man who is chafing under the irksomeness of his duty look to himself, and he will find that his wearisomeness proceeds, not from the duty itself, but from his selfish desire to escape it.

He who neglects duty, be it great or small, or of a public or private nature, neglects Virtue. He who in his heart rebels against duty, rebels against Virtue. When Duty becomes a thing of love, and when every particular duty is done accurately, faithfully, and dispassionately, there is much subtle selfishness removed from the heart, and a great step is taken towards the heights of Truth. The virtuous man concentrates his mind on the perfect doing of his own duty, and does not interfere with the duty of another.

The ninth step is the practice of Unswerving Rectitude or Moral Integrity. This Virtue must be firmly established in the mind, and so enter into every detail of a man's life. All dishonesty, deception, trickery, and misrepresentation must be forever put away, and the heart purged of every vestige of insincerity and deception. The least digression from the path of rectitude or righteousness is a deviation from Virtue.

There must be no extravagance and exaggeration of speech, but the simple truth should be stated. Engaging in deception, no matter how apparently insignificant, for boastful pride, or with the hope of personal advantage, is a state of delusion which one should make

efforts to dispel. It is demanded of the man of Virtue
that he shall not only practice the most rigid honesty
in thought, word, and deed, but that he shall be exact
in his statements, omitting and adding nothing to the
actual truth.

In thus shaping his mind to the principle of Rectitude or moral integrity, he will gradually come to
deal with people and things in a just and impartial
spirit, considering equity before himself, and view-
ing all things with freedom from personal bias, passion, and prejudice. When the Virtue of Rectitude is
fully practiced and comprehended, so that all temptation to untruthfulness and insincerity has ceased, then
is the heart made purer and nobler. Then is character
strengthened, and knowledge enlarged, and life takes
on a new meaning and a new power. Thus is the ninth
step accomplished.

The tenth step is the practice of Unlimited Forgiveness. This consists in overcoming the sense of injury
which springs from vanity, selfishness and pride; and
in exercising disinterested charity and large-hearted-
ness towards all. Spite, retaliation, and revenge are so
utterly ignoble, so base, and so small and foolish, as to
be altogether unworthy of being noticed or harbored.
No one who fosters such conditions in his heart can lift
himself above folly and suffering, and guide his life
aright. Only by casting them away, and ceasing to be
moved by them, can a man's eyes be opened to the true
way of life. Only by developing a forgiving and chari-

table spirit can he hope to approach and perceive the strength and beauty of a well-ordered life.

In the heart of the strongly virtuous man, no feeling of personal injury can arise. He has put away all retaliation, and has no enemies. If other men should regard themselves as his enemies, he will regard them kindly, understanding their ignorance, and making full allowance for it.

When this state of heart is arrived at, then the tenth step in the discipline of one's self-seeking inclinations is accomplished. Then the third great lesson in Virtue and Knowledge is learned and mastered.

Having thus laid down the first ten steps and three lessons in right-doing and right knowing, I leave those of my readers who are prepared for them to learn and master them in their everyday life.

There is, of course, a still higher discipline of the body, a more far-reaching discipline of the tongue, and greater and more all-embracing virtues to acquire and understand before the highest state of bliss and knowledge can be grasped. But it is not my purpose to deal with them here. I have expounded only the first and easiest lessons on the Higher Path, and by the time these are thoroughly mastered, the reader will have become so purified, strengthened, and enlightened, that he will not be left in the dark as to his future progress.

Those of my readers who have completed these three lessons will already have perceived, beyond and above, the high altitudes of Truth, and the narrow and precipitous track which leads to them, and will choose whether they shall proceed.

The straight Path which I have laid down can be pursued by all with greater profit to themselves and to the world. And even those who do not aspire to the attainment of Truth, will develop greater intellectual and moral strength, finer judgment, and deeper peace of mind by perfecting themselves in this Path. Nor will their material prosperity suffer by this change of heart; nay, it will be rendered truer, purer, and more enduring.

For if there is one who is capable of succeeding and fitted to achieve, it is the man who has abandoned the petty weaknesses and everyday vices of his kind, who is strong enough to rule his body and mind, and who pursues with fixed resolve the path of unswerving integrity and sterling virtue.

MENTAL CONDITIONS AND
THEIR EFFECTS

WITHOUT GOING into the details of the greater steps and lessons in the right life (a task outside the scope of this small work) a few hints concerning those mental conditions from which life in its totality springs seem in order. These hints will prove helpful to those who are ready and willing to penetrate further into the inner realm of heart and mind where Love, Wisdom, and Peace await the rapidly progressing student of life.

All sin is ignorance. It is a condition of darkness and undevelopment. The wrong thinker and the wrong-doer is in the same position in the school of life as the ignorant pupil in the school of learning. He has yet to learn how to think and act correctly, that is, in accordance with Law. The pupil in learning is not happy so long as he does his lessons wrongly. Likewise, unhappiness cannot be escaped while sin remains unconquered.

Life is a series of lessons. Some are diligent in learning them, and they become pure, wise, and altogether happy. Others are negligent, and do not apply themselves. They remain impure, foolish, and unhappy.

Every form of unhappiness springs from a wrong condition of mind. Happiness is inherent in right conditions of mind. Happiness is mental harmony, unhappiness is mental inharmony. While a man lives in wrong conditions of mind, he will live a wrong life, and will suffer continually.

Suffering is rooted in error. Bliss is inherent in enlightenment. There is salvation for man only in the destruction of his own ignorance, error, and self-delusion. Where there are wrong conditions of mind there is bondage and unrest. Where there are right conditions of mind there is freedom and peace.

Here are some of the leading wrong mental conditions and their disastrous effects upon one's life:

Wrong Mental Conditions	Their Effects
Hatred	Injury, violence, disaster, and suffering
Lust	Confusion of intellect, remorse, shame, and wretchedness
Covetousness	Fear, unrest, unhappiness, and loss.
Pride	Disappointment, humiliation, and lack of self-knowledge.
Vanity	Distress and mortification of spirit.
Condemnation	Persecution and hatred from others.
Ill-will	Failures and troubles.
Self-indulgence	Misery, loss of judgment, grossness, disease, and neglect.
Anger	Loss of power and influence.
Desire or Self-slavery	Grief, folly, sorrow, uncertainty, and loneliness.

The above wrong conditions of mind are merely negations. They are states of darkness and deprivation and not of positive power. Evil is not a power; it is ignorance and misuse of good. The hater is he who has failed to do the lesson of Love correctly, and he suffers in consequence. When he succeeds in doing it rightly, the hatred will have disappeared, and he will see and understand the darkness and impotence of hatred. This is so with every wrong condition.

The following are some of the more important right mental conditions and their beneficial effects upon one's life:

RIGHT MENTAL CONDITIONS	THEIR EFFECTS
Love	Gentle conditions, bliss, and blessedness.
Purity	Intellectual clearness, joy, invincible confidence.
Selflessness	Courage, satisfaction, happiness, and abundance.
Humility	Calmness, restfulness, knowledge of Truth.
Meekness	Emotional equilibrium, contentment under all circumstances.
Compassion	Protection, love, and reverence from others.
Goodwill	Gladness, success.
Self-control	Peace of mind, true judgment, refinement, health, and honor.
Patience	Mental power, far-reaching influence.
Self-conquest	Enlightenment, wisdom, insight, and profound peace.

The above right conditions of mind are states of positive power, light, joyful possession, and knowledge. The good man *knows*. He has learned to do his lessons correctly, and thereby understands the exact proportions which make up the sum of life. He is enlightened, and he knows good and evil. He is supremely happy, doing only that which is divinely right.

The man who is involved in the wrong conditions of mind, does not know. He is ignorant of good and evil, of himself, of the inward causes which make his life.

He is unhappy, and believes other people are entirely the cause of his unhappiness. He works blindly, and lives in darkness, seeing no central purpose in existence, and no orderly and lawful sequence in the course of things.

He who aspires to the attainment of the Higher Life in its completion—who would perceive with unveiled vision the true order of things and the meaning of life— let him abandon all the wrong conditions of the heart, and persevere unceasingly in the practice of good. If he suffers, or doubts, or is unhappy, let him search within until he finds the cause, and having found it, let him cast it away.

Let him so guard and purify his heart that every day less of evil and more of good shall issue therefrom. So he will daily become stronger, nobler, and wiser. So will his blessedness increase, and the Light of Truth, growing ever brighter and brighter within him, will dispel all gloom, and illuminate his Pathway.

EXHORTATION

DISCIPLES OF TRUTH, lovers of Virtue, seekers of Wisdom; you, also, who are sorrow stricken, knowing the emptiness of the self-life, and who aspire to the life that is supremely beautiful, and serenely joyful—take now yourselves in hand, enter the Door of Discipline, and know the Better Life.

Put away self-delusion. Behold yourself as you are, and see the Path of Virtue as it is. There is no lazy way to Truth. He who would stand upon the mountain's summit must strenuously climb, and must rest only to gather strength. But if the climbing is less glorious than the cloudless summit, it is still glorious. Discipline in itself is beautiful, and the end result of discipline is sweet.

Rise early and meditate. Begin each day with a conquered body, and a mind fortified against error and weakness. Temptation will never be overcome by unprepared fighting.

The mind must be armed and arrayed in the silent hour. It must be trained to perceive, to know, to understand. Sin and temptation disappear when right understanding is developed.

Right understanding is reached through unabated discipline. Truth cannot be reached but through discipline. Patience will increase by effort and practice, and patience will make discipline beautiful.

Discipline is irksome to the impatient man and the lover of self, so he avoids it, and continues to live loosely and confusedly.

Discipline is not irksome to the lover of Truth, and he will find the infinite patience which can wait, work, and overcome. Just as the joy of the gardener who sees his or her flowers develop day by day, so is the joy of the man of discipline who sees the divine flowers of Purity, Wisdom, Compassion, and Love, grow within his heart.

The loose-liver cannot escape sorrow and pain. The undisciplined mind falls, weak and helpless, before the fierce onslaught of passion.

Array well your mind, then, lover of Truth. Be watchful, thoughtful, and resolute. Your salvation is at hand; your readiness and effort are all that are needed. If you fail ten times, do not be disheartened. If you should fail a hundred times, rise up and pursue your way. If you should fail a thousand times, do not despair. When the right Path is entered, success is sure if the Path is not utterly abandoned.

First strife, and then victory. First labor, and then rest. First weakness, and then strength. In the beginning the lower life, and the glare and confusion of battle, and at the end the Life Beautiful, the Silence, and the Peace.

All common things, each day's events, That with the hour begin and end; Our pleasures and our discontents Are rounds by which we may ascend. We have not wings, we cannot soar; But we have feet to scale and climb.

—Longfellow

MORNING AND EVENING
THOUGHTS

| I | FIRST MORNING | I |

In aiming at the life of blessedness, one of the simplest beginnings to be considered, and rightly made, is that which we all make every day-namely, the beginning of each day's life. There is a sense in which every day may be regarded as the beginning of a new life, in which one can think, act, and live newly, and in a wiser and better spirit. The right beginning of the day will be followed by a cheerfulness permeating the household with a sunny influence, and the tasks and duties of the day will be undertaken in a strong and confident spirit, and the whole day will be well lived.

FIRST EVENING

There can be no progress, no achievement, without sacrifice, and a man's worldly success will be in the measure that he sacrifices his confused animal thoughts, and fixes his mind on the development of his plans, and the strengthening of his resolution and self-reliance. And the higher he lifts his thoughts, the more manly, upright, and righteous he becomes, the greater will be his success, the more blessed and enduring will be his achievements.

| 2 | SECOND MORNING | 2 |

None but right acts can follow right thoughts; none but a right life can follow right acts; and by living a right life all blessedness is achieved. Mind is the Master-power that moulds and makes. And Man is Mind, and evermore he takes. The Tool of thought, and, shaping what he wills, Brings forth a thousand joys, a thousand ills; He thinks in secret, and it comes to pass: Environment is but his looking-glass.

SECOND EVENING

Calmness of mind is one of the beautiful jewels of wisdom. A man becomes calm in the measure that he understands himself as a thought-evolved being. . . . And he as he develops a right understanding, and sees more and more clearly the internal relations of things by the action of cause and effect, he ceases to fret and fume, and worry and grieve, and remains poised, steadfast, serene.

3   THIRD MORNING   3

To follow, under all circumstances, the highest promptings within you; to be always true to the divine self; to rely upon the inward Voice, the inward Light, and to pursue your purpose with a fearless and restful heart, believing that the future will yield unto you the need of every thought and effort; knowing that the laws of the universe can never fail, and that your own will come back to you with mathematical exactitude-this is faith and the living of faith.

THIRD EVENING

Have a thorough understanding of your work, and let it be your own; and as you proceed, ever following the inward Guide, the infallible Voice, you will pass on from victory to victory, and will rise step by step to higher resting-places, and your ever- broadening outlook will gradually reveal to you the essential beauty and purpose of life. Self-purified, health will be yours; self-governed, power will be yours, and all that you do will prosper. And I may stand where health, success, and power Await my coming, if, each fleeting hour, I cling to love and patience; and abide With stainlessness; and never step aside From high integrity; so shall I see At last the land of immortality.

| 4 | FOURTH MORNING | 4 |

When the tongue is well controlled and wisely subdued; when selfish impulses and unworthy thoughts no longer rush to the tongue demanding utterance; when the speech has become harmless, pure, gracious, gentle, and purposeful, and no word is uttered but in sincerity and truth-then are the five steps in virtuous speech accomplished, then is the second great lesson in Truth learned and mastered. Make pure thy heart, and thou wilt make thy life Rich, sweet and beautiful.

FOURTH EVENING

Having clothed himself with humility, the first questions a man asks himself are:- "How am I acting towards others?" "What am I doing to others?" "How am I thinking of others?" "Are my thoughts of, and acts towards others prompted by unselfish love?" As a man, in the silence of his soul, asks himself these searching questions, he will unerringly see where he has hitherto failed.

| 5 | FIFTH MORNING | 5 |

To dwell in love always and towards all is to live the true life, is to have Life itself. Knowing this, the good man gives up himself unreservedly to the Spirit of Love, and dwells in Love towards all, contending with none, condemning none, but loving all. The Christ Spirit of Love puts an end, not only to all sin, but to all division and contention.

FIFTH EVENING

When sin and self are abandoned, the heart is restored to its imperishable Joy. Joy comes and fills the self-emptied heart; it abides with the peaceful; its reign is with the pure. Joy flees from the selfish, it deserts the quarrelsome; it is hidden from the impure. Joy cannot remain with the selfish; it is wedded to Love.

| 6 | SIXTH MORNING | 6 |

In the pure heart there is no room left where personal judgments and hatreds can find lodgment, for it is filled to overflowing with tenderness and love; it sees no evil, and only as men succeed in seeing no evil in others will they become free from sin, and sorrow, and suffering. If men only understood That the heart that sins must sorrow, That the hateful mind tomorrow Reaps its barren harvest, weeping, Starving, resting not, nor sleeping; Tenderness would fill their being, They would see with Pity's seeing If they only understood.

SIXTH EVENING

To stand face to face with truth; to arrive, after innumerable wanderings and pains, at wisdom and bliss; not to be finally defeated and cast out, but to ultimately triumph over every inward foe-such is man's divine destiny, such his glorious goal; and this, every saint, sage, and savior has declared. A man only begins to be a man when he ceases to whine and revile, and commences to search for the hidden justice which regulates his life. And as he adapts his mind to that regulating factor, he ceases to accuse others as the cause of his condition, and builds himself up in strong and noble thoughts; ceases to kick against circumstances, but begins to use them as aids to his more rapid progress, and as a means of discovering the hidden power and possibilities within himself.

| 7 | SEVENTH MORNING | 7 |

The will to evil and the will to good Are both within thee, which wilt thou employ? Thou knowest what is right and what is wrong, Which wilt though love and foster? which destroy? Thou art the chooser of thy thoughts and deeds; Thou art the maker of thine inward state; The power is thine to be what thou wilt be; Thou buildest Truth and Love, or lies and hate.

SEVENTH EVENING

The teaching of Jesus brings men back to the simple truth that righteousness, or right-doing, is entirely a matter of individual conduct, and not a mystical something apart from a man's thoughts and deeds. Calmness and patience can become habitual by first grasping, through effort, a calm and patient thought, and then continuously thinking it, and living in it, until "use becomes second nature," and anger and impatience pass away for ever.

8   ### EIGHTH MORNING   8

Man is made or unmade by himself; in the armoury of thought he forges the weapons by which he destroys himself; he also fashions the tools with which he builds for himself heavenly mansions of joy and strength and peace. By the right choice and true application of thought man ascends to the Divine Perfection; by the abuse and wrong application of thought he descends below the level of the beast. Between these two extremes are all the grades of character, and man is their maker and master. As a being of Power, Intelligence, and Love, and the lord of his own thoughts, man holds the key to every situation.

EIGHTH EVENING

Whatsoever you harbor in the inmost chambers of your heart will, sooner or later, by the inevitable law of reaction, shape itself in your outward life. Every soul attracts its own, and nothing can possibly come to it that does not belong to it. To realize this is to recognize the universality of Divine Law. If thou would'st right the world, And banish all its evils and its woes. Make its wild places bloom, And its drear deserts blossom as the rose- Then right thyself.

9   NINTH MORNING   9

Whatever conditions are rendering your life burdensome, you may pass out of and beyond them by developing and utilizing within you the transforming power of self-purification and self-conquest. Before the divine radiance of a pure heart all darkness vanishes and all clouds melt away, and he who has conquered self has conquered the universe. He who sets his foot firmly upon the path of self-conquest, who walks, aided by the staff of faith, the highway of self-sacrifice, will assuredly achieve the highest prosperity, and will reap abounding and enduring joy and bliss.

NINTH EVENING

It is the silent and conquering thought-forces which bring all things into manifestation. The universe grew out of thought. To adjust all your thoughts to a perfect and unswerving faith in the omnipotence and supremacy of Good, is to cooperate with that Good, and to realize within yourself the solution and destruction of all evil. To mentally deny evil is not sufficient; it must, by daily practice, be risen above and understood. To affirm the Good mentally is inadequate; it must, by unswerving endeavor, be entered into and comprehended.

10   TENTH MORNING   10

Every thought you think is a force sent out. Whatever your position in life may be, before you can hope to enter into any measure of success, usefulness, and power, you must learn how to focus your thought-forces by cultivating calmness and repose. There is no difficulty, however great, but will yield before a calm and purposeful concentration of thought, and no legitimate object but may be speedily actualized by the intelligent use and direction of one's soul forces. Think good thoughts, and they will quickly become actualized in your outward life in the form of good conditions.

TENTH EVENING

That which you would be and hope to be, you may be now. Non-accomplishment resides in your perpetual postponement, and, having the power to postpone, you also have the power to accomplish-to perpetually accomplish: realize this truth, and you shall be today, and every day, the ideal being of whom you dreamed. Say to yourself, "I will live in my Ideal now; I will manifest my ideal now; I will be my Ideal now; and all that tempts me away from my Ideal I will not listen to; I will listen only to the voice of my Ideal."

11   ELEVENTH MORNING   11

Be as a flower; content to be, to grow in sweetness day by day. If thou would'st perfect thyself in knowledge, perfect thyself in Love. If thou would'st reach the Highest, ceaselessly cultivate a loving and compassionate heart. To him who chooses Goodness, sacrificing all, is given that which is more than, and includes, all.

ELEVENTH EVENING

The Great Law never cheats any man of his just due. Human life, when rightly lived, is simple with a beautiful simplicity. He who comprehends the utter simplicity of life, who obeys its laws, and does not step aside into the dark paths and complex mazes of selfish desire, stands where no harm can reach him. Then there is fullness of joy, abounding plenty, and rich and complete blessedness.

12   TWELFTH MORNING   12

Every man reaps the results of his own thoughts and deeds, and suffers for his own wrong. He who begins right, and continues right, does not need to desire, and search for felicitous results; they are already at hand; they follow as consequences; they are the certainties, the realities, of life. Sweet is the rest and deep is the bliss of him who has freed his heart from its lusts and hatreds and dark desires.

TWELFTH EVENING

You are the creator of your own shadows; you desire, and then you grieve; renounce, and then you shall rejoice. Of all the beautiful truths pertaining to the soul, ... none is more gladdening or fruitful of divine promise and confidence than this-that man is the master of thought, the moulder of character, and the maker and shaper of character, environment, and destiny.

13   THIRTEENTH MORNING   13

As darkness is a passing shadow, and light is a substance that remains, so sorrow is fleeting, but joy abides for ever. No true thing can pass away and become lost; no false thing can remain and be preserved. Sorrow is false, and it cannot live; joy is true, and it cannot die. Joy may become hidden for a time, but it can always be recovered; sorrow may remain for a period, but it can be transcended and dispersed. Do not think your sorrow will remain; it will pass away like a cloud. Do not believe that the torments of sin are ever your portion; they will vanish like a hideous nightmare. Awake! Arise! Be holy and joyful.

THIRTEENTH EVENING

Tribulation lasts only so long as there remains some chaff of self which needs to be removed. The tribulum, or threshing machine, ceases to work when all the grain is separated from the chaff; and when the last impurities are blown away from the soul, tribulation has completed its work, and there is no more need for it; then abiding joy is realized. The sole and supreme use of suffering is to purify, to burn out all that is useless and impure. Suffering ceases for him who is pure. There could be no object in burning gold after the dross had been removed.

14   FOURTEENTH MORNING   14

In speaking of self-control, one is easily misunderstood. It should not be associated with a destructive repression, but with a constructive expression. A man is happy, wise and great in the measure that he controls himself; he is wretched, foolish, and mean in the measure that he allows his animal nature to dominate his thoughts and actions. he who controls himself, controls his life, his circumstances, his destiny; and wherever he goes he carries his happiness with him as an abiding possession. Renunciation precedes regeneration. The permanent happiness which men seek in dissipation, excitement, and abandonment to unworthy pleasures, is found only in the life which reverses all this- the life of self-control.

FOURTEENTH EVENING

Law, not confusion, is the dominating principle in the universe; justice, not injustice is the soul and substance of life; and righteousness, not corruption, is the moulding and moving force in the spiritual government of the world. This being so, man has but the right himself to find that the universe is right. When I am pure, I shall have solved the mystery of life; I shall be sure, When I am free from hatred, lust and strife, I am in Truth, and Truth abides in me; I shall be safe, and sane, and wholly free, When I am pure.

15   FIFTEENTH MORNING   15

If men only understood That their hatred and resentment Slays their peace and sweet contentment, Hurts themselves, helps not another, Does not cheer one lonely brother, They would seek the better doing Of good deeds which leaves no rueing. If they only understood. If men only understood How Love conquers; how prevailing Is its might, grim hate assailing; How compassion endeth sorrow, Maketh wise, and doth not borrow Pain of passion, they would ever Live in Love, in hatred never- If they only understood.

FIFTEENTH EVENING

The grace and beauty that were in Jesus can be of no value to you—cannot be understood by you—unless they are also in you, and they can never be in you, until you practise them, for, apart from doing, the qualities which constitute Goodness do not, as far as you are concerned, exist. To adore Jesus for his good qualities is a long step towards Truth, but to practise those qualities is Truth itself; and he who fully adores the perfection of another will not rest content in his own imperfection, but will fashion his soul after the likeness of that other. Therefore thou who adorest Jesus for his divine qualities, practise those qualities Thyself, and thou too shalt be divine.

16   SIXTEENTH MORNING   16

Let a man realize that life in its totality proceeds from the mind, and lo, the way of blessedness is opened up to him! For he will then discover that he possesses the power to rule his mind and to fashion it in accordance with his Ideal. So will he elect to strongly and steadfastly walk those pathways of thought and action which are altogether excellent; to him life will become beautiful and sacred; and, sooner or later, he will put to flight all evil, confusion, and suffering; for it is impossible for a man to fall short of liberation, enlightenment, and peace, who guards with unwearying diligence the gateway of his heart.

SIXTEENTH EVENING

By constantly overcoming self, a man gains a knowledge of the subtle intricacies of his mind; and it is this divine knowledge which enables him to become established in calmness. Without self-knowledge there can be no abiding peace of mind, and those who are carried away by tempestuous passions, cannot approach the holy place where calmness reigns. The weak man is like one who, having mounted a fiery steed, allows it to run away with him, and carry him withersoever it wills; the strong man is like one who, having mounted the steed, governs it with a masterly hand and makes it go in whatever direction and at whatever speed he commands.

17   SEVENTEENTH MORNING   17

There is no strife, no selfishness, in the Kingdom; there is perfect harmony, equipoise, and rest. Those who live in the Kingdom of Love, have all their needs supplied by the Law of Love. As self is the root cause of all strife And suffering, so Love is the root cause of all peace and bliss. Those who are at rest in the Kingdom, do not look for happiness in any outward possessions. They are freed from all anxiety and trouble and, resting in Love, they are the embodiment of happiness.

SEVENTEENTH EVENING

Let it not be supposed that the children of The Kingdom live in ease and indolence (these two sins are the first that have to be eradicated when the search for the Kingdom is entered upon); they live in a peaceful activity; in fact, they only truly live, for the life of self, with its train of worries, griefs, and fears, is not real life. The children of the Kingdom are Known by their life, they manifest the fruits of the Spirit-"Love, joy, peace, long-suffering, kindness, goodness, faithfulness, meekness, temperance, self-control"— under all circumstances and vicissitudes.

18   EIGHTEENTH MORNING   18

The gospel of Jesus is a gospel of living and doing. If it were not this it would not voice the Eternal Truth. Its Temple is Purified Conduct, the entrance-door to which is Self-surrender. It invites men to shake off sin, and promises, as a result, joy and blessedness and perfect peace. The Kingdom of Heaven is perfect trust, perfect knowledge, perfect peace. . . . No sin can enter therein, no self-born Thought or deed can pass its golden gates; no impure desire can defile its radiant robes. . . . All may enter it who will, but all must pay the price—the unconditional abandonment of self.

Eighteenth Evening

I say this—and know it to be truth—that circumstances can only affect you in so far as you allow them to do so. You are swayed by circumstances because you have not a right understanding of the nature, use, and power of thought. You believe (and upon this little word belief hang all our joys and sorrows) that outward things have the power to make or mar your life; by so doing you submit to those outward things, confess that you are their slave, and they your unconditional master. By so doing you invest them with a power which they do not of themselves possess, and you succumb, in reality not to the circumstances, but to the gloom or gladness, the fear or hope, the strength of weakness, which your thought-sphere has thrown around them.

19   Nineteenth Morning   19

If you are one of those who are praying for, and looking forward to a happier world beyond the grave, here is a message of gladness for you—you may enter into and realize that happy world now; it fills the whole universe, and it is within you, waiting for you to find, acknowledge, and possess. Said one who understood the inner laws of Being— "When men shall say, lo here, or lo there, go not after them. The Kingdom of God is within you."

Nineteenth Evening

Heaven and hell are inward states. Sink into self and all its gratifications, and you sink into hell; rise above self into that state of consciousness which is the utter denial and forgetfulness of self, and you enter heaven. So long as you persist in selfishly seeking for your own personal happiness, so long will happiness elude you, and you will be sowing the seeds of wretchedness. in so far as you succeed in losing yourself in the service of others, in that measure will happiness come to you, and you will reap a harvest of bliss.

20   TWENTIETH MORNING   20

Sympathy given can never be waste. One aspect of sympathy is that of Pity—pity for the distressed or pain-stricken, with a desire to alleviate or help them in their sufferings. The world needs more of this divine quality. "For pity makes the world Soft to the weak, and noble for the strong. Another form of sympathy is that of rejoicing with others who are more successful than ourselves, and though their success were our own.

TWENTIETH EVENING

Sweet are companionships, pleasures, and material comforts, but they change and fade away. Sweeter still are Purity, Wisdom, and the knowledge of Truth, and these never change nor fade away. He who attained to the possession of spiritual things can never be deprived of his source of happiness; he will never have to part company with it, and wherever he goes in the whole universe, he will carry his possessions with him. His spiritual end will be the fulness of joy.

21   TWENTY-FIRST MORNING   21

Let your heart grow and expand with ever- broadening love, until, freed from all hatred, and passion, and condemnation, it embraces the whole universe with thoughtful tenderness. As the flower opens its petals to receive the Morning-light, so open your soul more and more to the glorious light of Truth. Soar upward on the wings of aspiration; be fearless and believe in the loftiest possibilities.

Twenty-First Evening

Mind clothes itself in garments of its own making. Mind is the arbiter of life; it is the creator and shaper of conditions, and the recipient of its own results. It contains within itself both the power to create illusion and to perceive reality. Mind is the infallible weaver of destiny; thought is the thread, good and evil deeds are the warp and woof, and the web, woven upon the loom of life, is character. Make pure thy heart, and thou wilt make thy life Rich, sweet, and beautiful, unmarred by strife.

22   ## Twenty-Second Morning   22

Cherish your visions; cherish your ideals; cherish the music that stirs in your heart, the beauty that forms in your mind, the Loveliness that drapes your purest thoughts, for out of them will grow all delightful conditions, all heavenly environment; of these, if you will remain true to them, your world will at last be built. Guard well thy mind, and, noble, strong, and free, Nothing shall harm, disturb or conquer thee; For all thy foes are in thy heart and mind, There also thy salvation thou shalt find.

Twenty-Second Evening

Dream lofty dreams, and as you dream so shall you become. Your vision is the promise of what you shall one day be; your Ideal is the prophecy of what you shall at last unveil. The greatest achievement was at first and for a time a dream. The oak sleeps in the acorn; the bird waits in the egg; and in the highest vision of the soul a waking angel stirs. Your circumstances may be uncongenial, but they shall not long remain so when you perceive an Ideal and strive to reach it.

| 23 | TWENTY-THIRD MORNING | 23 |

He who has conquered doubt and fear has conquered failure. His every thought is allied with power, and all difficulties are bravely met and wisely overcome. His purposes are seasonably planted, and they bloom and bring forth fruit which does not fall prematurely to the ground. Thought allied fearlessly to purpose becomes creative force: he who knows this is ready to become something higher and stronger than a mere bundle of wavering thoughts and fluctuating sensations; he who does this has become the conscious and intelligent wielder of his mental powers.

TWENTY-THIRD EVENING

Man's true place in the Cosmos is that of a king, not a slave, a commander under the Law of Good, and not a helpless tool in the region of evil. I write for men, not for babes; for those who are eager to learn, and earnest to achieve; for those who will put away (for the world's good) a petty personal indulgence, a selfish desire, a mean thought, and live on as though it were not, sans craving and regret. Man is a master. If he were not, he could not act contrary to law. Evil and weakness are self destructive. The universe is girt with goodness and strength, and it protects the good and the strong. The angry man is the weak man.

| 24 | TWENTY-FOURTH MORNING | 24 |

Not by learning will a man triumph over evil; not by much study will he overcome sin and sorrow. Only by conquering himself will he conquer evil; only by practising righteousness will he put an end to sorrow. Not for the clever, nor the learned, nor the self-confident is the Life Triumphant, but for the pure, the virtuous and wise. The former achieve their particular success in life, but the latter alone achieve the great success so invincible and complete that even in apparent defeat it shines with added victory.

TWENTY-FOURTH EVENING

The true silence is not merely a silent tongue; it is a silent mind. To merely hold one's tongue, and yet to carry about a disturbed and rankling mind, is no remedy for weakness, and no source of power. Silentness, to be powerful, must envelop the whole mind, must permeate every chamber of the heart; it must be the silence of peace. To this broad, deep, abiding silentness a man attains only in the measure that he conquers himself.

25   TWENTY-FIFTH MORNING   25

By curbing his tongue, a man gains possession of his mind. The fool babbles, gossips, argues, and bandies words. He glories in the fact that he has had the last word, and has silenced his opponent. He exults in his own folly, is ever on the defensive, and wastes his energies in unprofitable channels. He is like a gardener who continues to dig and plant in unproductive soil. The wise man avoids idle words, gossips, vain argument, and self-defence. He is content to appear defeated; rejoices when he is defeated; knowing that, having found and removed another error in himself, he has thereby become wiser. Blessed is he who does not strive for the last word.

TWENTY-FIFTH EVENING

Desire is the craving for possession; aspiration is the hunger of the heart for peace. The craving for things leads ever farther and farther from peace, and not only ends in deprivation, but is in itself A state of perpetual want. Until it comes to an end, rest and satisfaction are impossible. The hunger for things can never be satisfied, but the hunger for peace can, and the satisfaction of peace is found—is fully possessed, when all selfish desire is abandoned. Then there is fullness of joy, abounding plenty, and rich and complete blessedness.

26   Twenty-Sixth Morning   26

A man will reach the Kingdom by purifying himself, and he can only do this by pursuing a process of self-examination and self-analysis. The selfishness must be discovered and understood before it can be removed. It is powerless to remove itself, neither will it pass away of itself. Darkness ceases only when light is introduced; so ignorance can only be dispersed by knowledge, selfishness by love. A man must first of all be willing to lose himself (his self-seeking) before he can find himself (his Divine Self). He must realize that selfishness is not worth clinging to, that it is a master altogether unworthy of his service, and that divine goodness alone is worthy to be enthroned in his heart, as the supreme master of his life.

Twenty-Sixth Evening

Be still, my soul, and know that peace is thine. Be steadfast, heart, and know that strength divine Belongs to thee; cease from thy turmoil, mind, And thou the Everlasting Rest shalt find. If a man would have peace, let him exercise the spirit of peace; if he would find Love, let him dwell in the spirit of Love; if he would escape suffering, let him cease to inflict it; if he would do noble things for humanity, let him cease to do ignoble things for himself. If he will but quarry the mine of his own soul, he shall find there all the materials for building whatsoever he will, and he shall find there also the Central Rock on which to build in safety.

27   Twenty-Seventh Morning   27

Men go after much company, and seek out new excitements, but they are not acquainted with peace; in divers paths of pleasure they search for happiness, but they do not come to rest; through divers ways of laughter and feverish delirium they wander after gladness and life, but their tears are many and grievous, and they do not escape death. Drifting upon the ocean of life in search of selfish indulgences, men are caught in its storms, and only after many tempests and much privation do they fly to the Rock of Refuge which rests in the deep silence of their own being.

Twenty-Seventh Evening

Meditation centered upon divine realities is the very essence and soul of prayer. It is the silent reaching upward of the soul toward the Eternal. Meditation is the intense dwelling, in thought, upon an idea or theme with the object of thoroughly comprehending it; and whatsoever you constantly meditate upon, you will not only come to understand, but will grow more and more into its likeness, for it will become incorporated with your very being, will become, in fact, your very self. If, therefore, you constantly dwell upon that which is selfish and debasing, you will ultimately become selfish and debased; if you ceaselessly think upon that which is pure and unselfish, you will surely become pure and unselfish.

28   Twenty-Eighth Morning   28

There is no difficulty, however great, but will yield before a calm and powerful concentration of thought, and no legitimate object but may be speedily actualized by the intelligent use and direction of one's soul forces. Whatever your task may be, concentrate your whole mind upon it; throw into it all the energy of which you are capable. The faultless completion of small tasks, leads inevitably to larger tasks. See to it that you rise by steady climbing, and you will never fall.

Twenty-Eighth Evening

He who knows that Love is at the heart of all things, and has realized the all-sufficing power of that Love, has no room in his heart for condemnation. If you love people and speak of them with praise, until they in some way thwart you, or do something of which you disapprove, and then you dislike them and speak of them with dispraise, you are not governed by the Love which is of God. If, in your heart, you are continually arraigning and condemning others, selfless love is hidden from you. Train your mind in strong, impartial, and gentle thought; train your heart in purity and compassion; train your tongue to silence, and to true and stainless speech; so shall you enter the way of holiness and peace, and shall ultimately realize the immortal Love.

29   TWENTY-NINTH MORNING   29

If you would realize true prosperity, do not settle down, as many have done, into the belief that if you do right everything will go wrong. Do not allow the word "Competition" to shake your faith in the supremacy of righteousness. I care not what men say about the "laws of competition," for do not I know the Unchangeable Law which shall one day put them all to rout, and which puts them to rout even now in the heart and life of the righteous man? And knowing this law I can contemplate all dishonesty with undisturbed repose, for I know where certain destruction awaits it. Under all circumstances do that which you believe to be right, and trust the Law; trust the Divine Power which is immanent in the universe, and it will never desert you, and you will always be protected.

TWENTY-NINTH EVENING

Forget yourself entirely in the sorrows of others, and in ministering to others, and divine happiness will emancipate you from all sorrow and suffering. "Taking the first step with a good thought, the second with a good word, and the third with a good deed, I entered Paradise." And you also enter Paradise by pursuing the same course. Lose yourself in the welfare of others; forget yourself in all that you do—this is the secret of abounding happiness. Ever be on the watch to guard against selfishness and learn faithfully the divine lessons of inward sacrifice; so shall you climb the highest heights of happiness, and shall remain in the never-clouded sunshine of universal joy, clothed in the shining garment of immortality.

30   THIRTIETH MORNING   30

When the farmer has tilled and dressed his land and put in the seed, he knows that he has done all that he can possibly do, and that now he must trust to the elements, and wait patiently for the course of time to bring about the harvest, and that no amount of expectancy on his part will affect the result. Even so, he who has realized Truth, goes forth as a sower of the seeds of goodness, purity, love, and peace, without expectancy and never looking for results, knowing that there is the Great Overruling Law which brings about its own harvest in due time, and which is alike the source of preservation and destruction.

THIRTIETH EVENING

The virtuous put a check upon themselves, and set a watch upon their passions and emotions; in this way they gain possession of the mind, and gradually acquire calmness; and as they acquire influence, power, greatness, abiding joy, and fullness and completeness of life. He only finds peace who conquers himself, who strives, day by day, after greater self-possession, greater self-control, greater calmness of mind. Where the calm mind is there is strength and rest, there is love and wisdom; there is one who has fought successfully innumerable battles against self, who, after long toil in secret against his own failings, has triumphed at last.

Sympathy bestowed increases its store in our own heart and enriches and fructifies our own life. Sympathy given is blessedness received; sympathy withheld is blessedness forfeited. In the measure that a man increases and enlarges his sympathy so much nearer does he approach the ideal life, the perfect blessedness; and when his heart has become so mellowed that no hard, bitter, or cruel thought can enter, and detract from its permanent sweetness, then indeed is he richly and divinely blessed.

THIRTY-FIRST EVENING

Sweet is the rest and deep the bliss of him who has freed his heart from its lusts and hatreds and dark desires; and he who, without any shadow of bitterness resting upon him, and looking out upon the world with boundless compassion and love, can breathe, in his inmost heart, the blessing: Peace unto all living things, making no exceptions or distinctions—such a man has reached that happy ending which can never be taken away, for this is the perfection of life, the fulness of peace, the consummation of perfect blessedness.

Made in United States
Troutdale, OR
12/05/2024

25866077R00065